RETOX

RETOX

BOOZE, USE, AND SNOOZE YOUR WAY TO PERSONAL FULFILLMENT

By Jennifer Traig and Victoria Traig

Illustrations by Maria Raymondsdotter

CHRONICLE BOOKS

SAN FRANCISCO

Library of Congress Cataloging-in-Publication Data:

Traig, Jennifer.
  Retox: booze, use, and snooze your way to personal fulfillment/
by Jennifer Traig and Victoria Traig.
      p. cm.
  ISBN-10: 0-8118-5329-2
  ISBN-13: 978-0-8118-5329-3
  1. Alcoholism–Humor. 2. Drug abuse–Humor. 3. Food habits–Humor.
  4. Conduct of life–Humor. I. Traig, Victoria. II. Title.
  PN6231.A448T73 2006
  818'.602–dc22

                                    2005027437

Manufactured in Canada.
Designed by Mark Wasserman at Plinko.

Distributed in Canada by Raincoast Books
9050 Shaughnessy Street
Vancouver, British Columbia V6P 6E5

10 9 8 7 6 5 4 3 2 1

Chronicle Books LLC
85 Second Street
San Francisco, California 94105
www.chroniclebooks.com

TABLE OF CONTENTS

INTRO-DUCTION

You've detoxed. You've simplified your life. You've cleansed your colon and searched your soul. You meditate. You think about your bowels a lot. You spend far too much time in nature and other places that don't have cocktail service. For fun, you rub yourself with crystals, cleanse your chi, align your chakras, and munch on foods with all the fiber content and flavor of sawdust. You are as pure as filtered water, and just as interesting. Admit it: you're bored. Worse, you're boring. Your friends have stopped calling you. Your coworkers won't return your e-mail. Even the Sierra Club canvassers are reluctant to ring your doorbell after your self-righteous "save the wetlands" tirade. Well, tirade no more. *Retox* is here to help you get back the highly entertaining, screwed-up life you had before you became perfect.

Listen to us: Protein bars are not a substitute for *candy*. Soy yogurt is not a substitute for butter eaten straight from the stick. Chai is not a substitute for the really good over-the-counter muscle relaxants you have to go to Mexico to get. And, dammit, wheatgrass juice is *not a shot*. It's just what happens when you accidentally leave the sprinklers on all night. People. Please.

It's a good thing we're here. Maybe you're starting off on a high horse. Or maybe you've already hit bottom. Whatever your background—high life, no life—we'll help you navigate the low life. We will shepherd you through dives, doughnut shops, medicine cabinets, and carnie clubs. In no time at all, the gutter will feel like home.

Think of this as alternative medicine, as homeopathics gone wild. Exposure will build up your immunity. Your body will become comfortable and familiar with the likes of whiskey, tranquilizers, and tobacco in all its forms. And goodness knows it could use a corn dog. Low-fat diets have been linked with depression. We'll get that dangerously low cholesterol level back up above three hundred where it belongs.

It may not be good for you, and it might land you in jail, but we can promise you this: your new life will be fun. You can take the money you pledged to PBS and spend it on Slurpees and Lotto tickets instead. You don't have to recycle anymore. Bye-bye, chamomile tea! So long, tofu! You can stay out all night, call in sick to work, and watch the Home Shopping Network all day. Enjoy the satisfaction of reconstructing the events of the previous night using the string of clues you find on your bedside table. Remember: you can't spell dysfunction without f-u-n!

Before long the changes will show. The glow of health will give way to the ruddy big-pored sheen of the career partyer. Your yoga pants and polar fleece will be replaced by leather trousers whose pockets are full of unfamiliar phone numbers. You'll look like trouble, and you'll wear it well. Muss up your hair and tuck your skirt hem into your underwear, and in no time the paparazzi will be mistaking you for Courtney Love.

Get ready to be America's sweetheart. You're going to be in high demand. You'll win back those friends you lost going on about your juice fast when you thrill them with tales of that seventy-two-hour hot tub party. You'll be the talk of the town when you show up at work with your shirt on inside out and a devilish grin on your face. You'll become a Page Six staple, described as "the notorious" so often you'll start to think it's your first name.

You've got a lot of debauching to do, so let's get started. Warn the local authorities, stock up on analgesics, and put your lawyer on speed dial, because we're about to have some fun.

Cheers!

A DIS-CLAIMER

Unless years of inhalant abuse have already taken their toll, it should go without saying that this is intended as a humor book and not an actual lifestyle guide. This book is full of dangerous suggestions, foolish advice, and across-the-board bad ideas (except for the deep-fried Twinkies, which are excellent). The authors would like to clarify to anyone who might be reading this, especially their parents, that they've never tried any of the activities described herein, especially not the illegal or narcotic ones. Except for the deep-fried Twinkies, which, again, are excellent. Enjoy.

HEALTH AND WELL-BEING

1

The Retox plan begins on the cellular level with a total-body overhaul. Here is where you'll learn to undo all the stinkin' thinkin' you've absorbed over the years about healthy living and homeopathic medicine. Our carefully designed regime of pills, junk food, booze, and tobacco will reverse the long-term effects of good nutrition and regular exercise in a matter of days. If you're a binger, you could see results in hours. Far more effective than acupuncture, and not a total crock like Reiki, it's designed to produce real change. You'll be amazed at how much better you feel. Stress? Gone. Anxiety? Poof. Your wallet and keys? Hmm, those seem to be missing too. Who cares? We're having a good time! So get ready for a whole new you—a *fun* you. And isn't fun worth a persistent cough and inexplicably shaky hands?

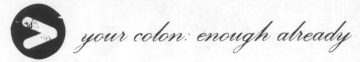 *your colon: enough already*

When did irrigating one's bowels become a pastime of the rich and neurotic instead of the elderly and constipated? A high colonic is not a *spa treatment*. It is not a fashion accessory. It's an enema and should be performed only on invalids and children who've swallowed valuable jewelry. And another thing: it is not *therapy*. Yes, you have problems. But an enema is not going to get rid of them. So stop abusing your poor intestines with fiber and coffee pumped in the wrong way. We're here to help you get things back on track. To undo the damage you've done with those week-long power cleanses, we present our reverse colonic. This seven-day plan will help you build up a helpful lining of toxins, goo, and detritus that will keep the really bad stuff from getting absorbed directly into your bloodstream. Our colonic goes in the *right* way, and the regimen of limited activity and gentle, binding foods will give your colon the week off. Maybe two.

BACK IN THE SADDLE AGAIN
THE RETOX REVERSE COLONIC

Day 1

Like most colonic regimens, this one begins with a liquid fast. No, no, we don't mean that awful lemon juice-cayenne-and-maple syrup liquid. We mean booze. Put the "high" in "high colonic" with a steady stream of cocktails. Liquor will kill any bad critters your so-called "cleansing" may have left you susceptible to, and it'll help your colon relax. Because many people find that herbs enhance the process, elixirs like Jägermeister, Benedictine, and mint juleps are ideal.

Day 2

Slowly introduce foods. For today, you may eat anything normally found in a bar or at the nearby gas station vending machine. You'll want to avoid anything with fiber. Any fruit associated with a cocktail is OK, and whipped cream is ideal.

Day 3

Continue with liquids and gentle solids. Since your diet will be limited at this point, you'll want to be sure to include dietary supplements. We recommend Vicodin. It's loaded with healthy opiates, and the mild constipating effect is only a bonus.

Day 4

Be careful to avoid physical activity; you don't want to accidentally knock anything loose. In lieu of exercise, keep your heart rate up with lots of coffee. It goes without saying that it should enter your body *through your mouth*.

Day 5

Today you'll introduce cheese, and plenty of it.

Day 6

Swallow some gum. We're not sure we really believe that it stays in your stomach for seven years, but, just in case it does, it's probably good to build a little stockpile of Juicy Fruit in there, to give your stomach something to do when you don't have time to eat.

Day 7

Has it been seven days already? That can't be right. Why, we started with a full bottle of Vicodin, and let's see, doing the math, six of those little guys a day times seven days means today is, hoo, we are in no condition to do math right now. OK! Day seven it is! The reverse colonic is over, and a brave little soldier you were. Nice work. Now get out there and make up for lost time. The world is your oyster, and it needs some Tabasco.

the home pharmacist's table of equivalents

Say good-bye to the herbalist and hello to the magical world of pharmacology. Prescription drugs truly make our lives better, and we know you'll come to love them like we do in no time at all. We give thanks every single day that we live in an era of rampant overprescription and twenty-four-hour pharmacies. If you play your cards right, you should be able to feel nothing but chemically generated emotions most of your natural-born life. But no matter how well you plan, there will still be times when mother finds herself without her little helper. Maybe Dr. Feelgood finally got wise to your editorial revisions to his refill instructions, or maybe www.mexicanpharmacist.com is having server problems. Well, don't you worry (as if you could, with all the residual Xanax in your body). These handy homemade substitutions will see you through until you can "borrow" another prescription pad.

Adderall = 2 cans Red Bull + 1 tab Dristan Severe Cold Formula + butt-rock CD

Ambien = 1 tab Benadryl + rerun of *The Actors' Studio*

Ativan = 1 cup stress tea + 10 minutes meditation and yogic breathing + giving up and drinking $1/2$ bottle Jameson's, straight

Demerol = $1/2$ bottle Jameson's, straight

Klonopin = 2 tabs Dramamine + 1 bottle Night Train

Ortho Tri-Cyclen = 3 tabs Estroven + parking ticket + bounced check + fight with partner + entire can of Pringles

Oxycontin = $1/4$ cup Nyquil + mild concussion

Percocet = 3 tabs Extra Strength Tylenol + ground-up dust found in jacket pocket that might be old Vicodin residue

Phen-Fen = 3 tabs TrimSpa + 2 pieces Nicorette (Repeat dosage until you feel symptoms of mild heart attack.)

Propecia = 1 tab One-A-Day Men's Health Formula + 10 drops Miracle-Gro (This formula may also be substituted for Viagra.)

Prozac = 1 tab Saint-John's-wort + Miller Lite + IRS audit of evil former employer

Retin-A = Paint stripper + Oil of Olay (topical use only)

Ritalin = 4 cans Diet Coke + Dexatrim + 2 days' sleep deprivation + baby laxative

Valium = 40-ounce bottle of Olde English 800 + 2 tablespoons Robitussin + *The Best of Burt Bacharach*

Wellbutrin = gin gimlet + Internet shopping spree (minimum of

HOMEMADE TRANSDERMAL NICOTINE PATCHES

Looking for a convenient, portable, twenty-four-hour hands-free supply of sweet, sweet nicotine? The patch is heaven sent. The only downside? It can get pricey, especially if you're wearing three or four at a time. Why throw away your money when you can make the patch for just a few pennies? Here's how:

Simply take a handful of chewing tobacco, and affix to your skin with duct tape!

Experiment with different flavors. Wintergreen will make you smell minty fresh *and* soothe your aching muscles with the power of menthol. Skoal Vanilla? Sexy!

DO IT YOURSELF BOTOX

No time to run to the dermatologist's office? Tired of shelling out $500 a pop? Sick of granite eyebrows and uncontrollable drooling? Then home Botox is for you. Totally temporary and cheap, cheap, cheap, it delivers all the benefits of Botox with none of the drawbacks. And all you need is a box of Band-Aids.

Simply place Band-Aid over deeply-carved eyebrow furrow and leave in place. You can tell people you had a tweezing accident. Where's the wrinkle now? We can't see it at all!

For an instant face lift, pull skin back at temples and hold in place with more Band-Aids. You'll look ten years younger! Use Muppet Band-Aids, and you'll look *thirty* years younger!

self-medication: yes, you can

There's a common misconception that you need a medical background to diagnose and treat yourself. *Au contraire, mon frère.* If so-called "naturopaths" and "holistic healers" can practice medicine, there's no reason you can't. In fact, the less you know, the better. Facts and truths will only cloud your judgment. Remember, self-diagnosis is an art, not a science. And self-medication is just a plain old good time. Following are some common afflictions and their corresponding treatments. You may need to customize your Rx to suit your particular tastes. Please refer to the Home Pharmacist's Table of Equivalents (page 18) if you can't readily (or legally) acquire the treatment you seek. Remember, follow your gut, not your brain.

Irritable Bowel Syndrome

Symptoms: Alternating constipation and diarrhea, and general restlessness down below

Treatment: 2 tablespoons Pepto-Bismol + 1 chili dog (You're already feeling all messed up, so you might as well enjoy yourself.)

Irritable Boss Syndrome

Symptoms: Suddenly your three-hour lunches and pilfering of office supplies are deemed unacceptable.

Treatment: Spiking coffee with rum at work + blaming pilfering of office supplies on coworker who ratted you out in the first place

Huge Zit

Symptoms: Huge zit

Treatment: 1 bottle cheap wine + visit from friend with worse zit

Bad Haircut

Symptoms: Bad haircut

Treatment: 1 bottle Jose Cuervo + sombrero

Buyer's Remorse

Symptoms: Feelings of guilt related to recent purchase

Treatment: 2 cocktails + 1 reassuring friend + second shopping spree that makes your initial one seem like child's play

Extended Family Visit

Symptoms: Family members are at your house much, much longer than they should be.

Treatment: 1 tab Ativan (or equivalent—see page 18) every 4 hours + cessation of all hygiene

Headache

Symptoms: Headaches

Treatment: 1 Irish coffee + 2 tabs Vicodin + 3 tabs Percocet (Sure, a couple ibuprofen would probably do the trick, but you don't want to take any chances with the old noggin.)

Weight Gain (Real, Imagined, or Supermodel Induced)

Symptoms: Snug clothes; nights spent alone eating Milanos

Treatment: Night of binge drinking followed by morning of vigorous vomiting (it's exercise!). Repeat until desired body weight is achieved.

Suspicious Mole

Symptoms: Dark mole that you could swear is changing size and color

Treatment: Panic, call friend, take Xanax, then decide it's probably a pimple after learning your HMO has upped your copay once again.

Impending Cold Sore

Symptoms: Tingling around the mouth two days before important social event

Treatment: Borrow a friend's matte lipstick to conceal and sop up the ooze.

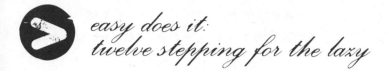

easy does it: twelve stepping for the lazy

There's no denying that the traditional twelve-step method is effective. It's also a whole lot of work. Personal inventories, righting wrongs, making amends—it's a full-time job, and not a very interesting one either. Step, step, step . . . all that climbing makes us wonder why you don't just take the escalator instead. It is in this spirit that we present our super-simplified EZ twelve-step alternative. It's so easy that it only has eleven steps! We saved you one right there! Will it work? Probably not. Could it make things much worse? Definitely. But it's fast and simple, and if you talk a lot about your "steps" you just might trick your family into calling off the intervention they've been planning. Easy Does It!

Step 1: The traditional first step is to admit your life has become unmanageable. No problem there. But rather than actually change it, why not just hire someone to manage it? She will clean up after your drunken rampages, call in sick to work for you when you're too hung over, and send apology notes to the people you accidentally hit on while drunk. A *functional* alcoholic—now that's a step up!

Steps 2 and 3: These steps require you to turn your life over to your higher power. Hey, if we read that as "hire power"— which is pretty much what we did when we *hired* the personal assistant in step 1—then we've already done that. Two birds with one stone! Now we have more time to drink! Yay!

Step 4: Well, you're *supposed* to make a fearless moral inventory of yourself, but that doesn't sound like much fun. You know what does, though? Making a fearless moral inventory of others. Sit down and list all your friends' faults. We're not quite sure what this will accomplish, but it can easily be done while watching reality TV shows and drinking Pabst, so why not?

Step 5: Here, you're supposed to confess your wrongdoings to another person. Let's make it easier: just confess your fashion faux pas. It's OK. Let it all out—the leather pants, the platform boots, the scrunchies, all of it. You're only as sick as your worst outfit.

Step 6: This one involves something about removing defects of character. That sounds hard. Let's take a break! Taking a break is the new step 6!

Step 7: Let's make it a long break!

Step 8:   Make a list of everyone you've harmed. Are we crazy, or does that actually sound entertaining? Remember the time you accidentally took $200 out of your brother's wallet, leaving him so short on cash that he couldn't pay rent, lost his apartment, and had to move in with your parents? That was *hysterical*. Good times.

Step 9:   Step 9, tough version: make amends. Step 9, Retox version: make Tater Tots! They only take twenty minutes, and nothing says "I'm sorry I ran over your dog" like a plate of piping-hot fried potatoes.

Step 10:   You're supposed to take a personal inventory and admit when you were wrong. Instead, what say you just inventory your CDs and admit that some of them suck? Hey, remember when you had a whiskey drink and a vodka drink and decided it would be a good idea to buy the Chumbawamba CD? That *sucked*.

Step 11:   This step involves meditation and prayer. You know what's a lot like meditation? Napping. Let's take a nap instead. After slogging your way through the previous steps, you've earned one. And a nightcap, too.

ENABLER STABLE

No functional alcoholic can do it alone. Like a champion thoroughbred, you need a support crew. There are five types of stablemates every Retox horse needs in order to win the race:

The Drinking Buddy

The drinking buddy drinks a lot—even more than you. He will encourage you to drink, make you feel like the amount you consume is moderate, and pick up the occasional tab, especially when he's too wasted to remember picking up the last three.

The Yes Man

The yes man is the friend who is loyal to the end. She will tell you you're OK when no one else will, and she'll always give the right answer. "Do I look good in these leather chaps?" Yes, you do. "Should I have one more drink to make it an even ten?" Yes, you should. Have you found a friend for life? Yes, you have.

The Garbage Man

This is the friend who helps clean up your messes. He will not shy away from your drama or your vomit. He will hide the empties before you've even woken up. He will smooth over your alcohol-fueled arguments and bail you out of jail. He's a problem solver, and you're his favorite problem.

The Nanny

The nanny is your go-to gal when you need a little mothering. She'll hold your hair while you puke, drag your lifeless body from the bathroom floor and tuck you snugly into bed (making sure to position you on your side), and call in sick for you the next morning. Best of all, she knows that tequila, not laughter, is the best medicine.

38467210

38467211

38467212

38467214

2

DIET

So how's that diet working out for you? It sure looks like you're having fun, and it's certainly made you a *fascinating* person. No, really, please—tell us again how many carbs you had yesterday. Only three? Go on.

We can't help noticing, however, that your new lifestyle seems to be an awful lot of work. Keeping track of your points, figuring out your fat-protein-carb ratios, screaming at waitresses who forget to remove the bun—how you manage to find time to lecture us about buying nonorganic produce, we don't know. And while we're noticing: why do you still wear a T-shirt in the pool? All that work and you still hate your body. Sigh.

Well, sweetie, it's time to pack your bags, because we're getting you out of South Beach. You're on the Retox regime now. Think of it as the Zone in reverse. It's the Twilight Zone, a world without rules where you learn to love your body by giving it exactly what it wants. Binge, purge—it all works out in the end. So forget the diets and bodywork and just do what feels good. Instead of Reiki, steaky. Instead of rolfing, ralphing. Trade your sticky mats for sticky buns, your ab crunches for Nestlé crunches. And you can say good-bye to health food stores, with their high prices and brewer's yeast stink. All the foods on the Retox plan can be found in vending machines, gas stations, and mini-marts. And since the low-protein and high-fat content of convenience foods will cause you to lose muscle mass, and muscle weighs more than fat, you'll actually *lose weight.* Bon appétit!

retox power foods from a to z

Sure, berries are loaded with cancer-fighting antioxidants, and fish prevents heart disease, but neither of them will get you through your boss's micromanagement deadline freak-out or a weekend with your passive-aggressive mother-in-law. When you need some *real* energy, turn to the energizing edibles below. Unlike organic produce and herbal concoctions, they're cheap, tasty, and widely available—heck, some aren't even *food*—ideal for the power eater on the go!

Appletini: An apple a day keeps the doctor away. But an appletini (or four) will keep *all* your problems away. Until tomorrow morning, anyway, but we won't worry about that now. To your health!

Beef jerky: Want to look well preserved? Down this preservative-rich snack. Eat enough of it and they won't even need to embalm you.

Cake mix: Don't worry about actually baking it—you can eat this carb cocaine straight out of the box with a wet fingertip, just like you did under the covers every night in sixth grade when your friends started to hate you. And didn't it make you feel better?

Dexedrine: A favorite of the 1950s sorority girl, Dexedrine will get you through that teeth-grinding lunch with Mummy. You won't need to even touch your food!

Entenmann's: Nobody understands you like Dr. E does.

Frozen pound cake: Yeah, right, like you're going to wait for it to thaw after the day you've had.

Gravy: Meaty goodness in convenient liquid form.

Hostess snack cakes: The original PowerBar, snack cakes pack plenty of energizing glucose and trans fats into a compact, portable package. Occasionally blamed for assassinations.

Ice: Stressed out? Between the potato chips and the Cheetos, crunch on some ice for instant relaxation. It'll give your teeth (and your dental insurance) a workout!

Jalapeño poppers: The most macho of all deep-fried appetizers. *¡Que fuerza!*

Krispy Kremes: That a food can be (a) crème filled, (b) glazed, and (c) deep-fried all at once makes us proud to be American. It is simply not possible to cram more empty calories into one package. Take that, Russia!

Lip gloss: Because you can't eat *broccoli* off your lips when you're feeling insecure.

Mountain Dew: If you've ever drunk a two-liter bottle of this stuff for a 4:00 A.M. breakfast behind the wheel of a semi, then you know first-hand the power this potion packs.

Nyquil: If you've ever drunk a two-liter bottle of Mountain Dew for a 4:00 A.M. breakfast behind the wheel of a semi and then needed to relax enough to cram in a three-hour power nap before heading back down to Mexicali, you probably drank a whole lot of Nyquil. And it probably worked great.

Olde English 800: It's four times more powerful than Olde English 200, and it packs 40 ounces of malt liquor muscle.

Pudding: Like an emotional Band-Aid you can eat with a spoon.

Quaaludes: The Rohypnol of its day, this stuff has been hard to come by since it was banned in the 1970s, but it's worth the search. Try going through your black-sheep aunt's disco purses to see if there's an expired tab or two. There's a reason they made these illegal!

Red pistachios: The red powder provides extra nutritive redness.

Sour grapes: What's more motivating than the acrid taste of another person's success?

Taquitos: All the nutrition of a taco in a smaller, easy-to-eat package. It's like a deep-fried meat-filled cigar!

Ultra-strength ibuprofen: It's not Vicodin, but two of these and a glass of wine will get you halfway there.

Vanilla frosting: Provides all the glucose of those creepy marathoner goo packs with none of the ass taste.

Wintergreen breath mints: The at-work drinker's best friend.

Xanax: Chamomile tea may be soothing, but it won't get you through tax time/the holidays/cross-country travel like this little pill will. Thank you, Eli Lilly!

Yoo-hoo: The diesel in New York City's tank, Yoo-hoo fuels the go-getter on the run.

Zonkers, Screaming Yellow: They are yellow, and they scream. That's all you need to know.

tongue shui: the tao of frying

We're not quite sure why deep-fat frying gets such a bad rap. Sure, the calories and saturated fat are a one-way ticket to a quintuple bypass, but it's not *all* bad. Frying makes everything taste good—even inedible compost fodder like vegetables. More important, it infuses foods with healthy, depression-fighting fat molecules. It's good for you! Sort of!

We need only look to our friends in the Far East for proof. After all, the same culture that invented acupuncture and Zen dreamed up the wonton and the spring roll. The Chinese fry everything, even rice, and they're about a billion times healthier and better adjusted than we are. So fire up the Fry Daddy and come to Papa. Confucius say: Steaming is shallow. Frying is deep.

We like to call it tongue shui, Eastern philosophy for your mouth. Like feng shui, frying incorporates five different elements. Embrace its teachings.

THE FIVE ELEMENTS OF FRYING

1. Hot oil . . . . fire
2. Batter coating . . . . earth
3. Stick . . . . wood
4. Slotted spoon . . . metal
5. Ketchup . . . water

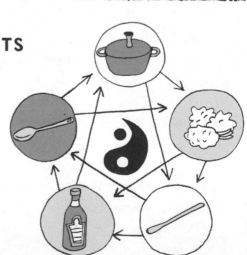

FRYING WISDOM

You cannot unfry, but you can refry.

Frying enriches the humblest morsel.

In every life, there is splatter.

THE FOUR JUSTIFICATIONS

1. It can't absorb all that much oil.

2. You'll have salad for dinner.

3. It's probably better for you than bacon (oh, wait, that *is* bacon).

4. It will give you a shiny coat.

FRYKU

It's a frying haiku. Try writing your own!

Golden Tater Tots

Dancing in hot bubbling oil

I eat you with ranch

HERE ARE SOME THINGS YOU MIGHT ENJOY FRYING

Frozen burritos

Snickers bars

Twinkies

Cheesecake

HERE ARE SOME THINGS YOU WILL NOT

Yogurt

Molasses

Lettuce

 *sample menus*

The Retox diet plan is very basic: eat what you want when you want. Waffles for dinner? Why not? Doritos for breakfast? Yes, please. The idea is to erase any preconceived notions you might have about proper nutrition, and tune in to your snacking intuition. Listen to your belly. It knows what your body needs. Do you think it's a coincidence that scurvy-stricken sailors craved screwdrivers and lemon bars? Of course not.

It is entirely possible to eat what you crave without any risk of obesity. There are two ways to achieve this state of dietary bliss. Menu A involves cutting out certain foods (like fruits and vegetables) in order to keep your caloric intake below 2,000 a day. Menu B allows you to eat to your heart's desire while adding dietary supplements such as laxatives, diuretics, and speed. Either way, you lose!

day one

MENU A

Breakfast:
- One 2³/₄-ounce bag Doritos
- 1 can diet Mountain Dew

Lunch:
- 1 bag uncooked ramen noodles, licked and then dipped into seasoning packet
- 1 bottle Sunny Delight

Dinner:
- *I Love New York Dinner Special:* 2 Krispy Kremes and a Manhattan

MENU B

Breakfast:
- One 13¹/₂-ounce bag Doritos
- 1 can Mountain Dew

Lunch:
- 4 bags uncooked ramen noodles, licked and then dipped into seasoning packet
- 12 ounces Sunny Delight topped with whipped cream

Dinner:
- *I Love New York Dinner Special Supreme:* 2 dozen Krispy Kremes and a pitcher of Manhattans

Supplement:
- 4 Ex-Lax pills

day two

MENU A

Breakfast:
- Bagel with light cream cheese
- Half-drunk wine cooler from night before

Lunch:
- *The Captain's Table:* 1 bowl Cap'n Crunch 1 shot Captain Morgan

Dinner:
- *3 Men and a Baby:* 1 Manwich sandwich, 1 mandarin orange, 1 Manhattan, and 1 Baby Ruth

MENU B

Breakfast:
- Chocolate-chip and cream-cheese bagel sandwich
- Half-drunk case of wine coolers from night before

Lunch:
- *The Captain's Table:* 1 box Cap'n Crunch 1 bottle Captain Morgan

Dinner:
- *Six Men and Two Babies:* 2 Manwich sandwiches, 1 mandarin orange, 3 Manhattans, and 2 Baby Ruths

Supplement:
- 13 diuretics (your choice)

day three

MENU A

Breakfast:
- Olive, lime, and celery kabob
- Bloody Mary (in which the above are immersed)

Lunch:
- 1 peanut butter and SPAM sandwich
- 1 cup Kool-Aid, spiked with grain alcohol

Dinner:
- *Vive La France Carb Fest:* French toast, French fries, and French bread. *Sacre bleu!*

MENU B

Breakfast:
- 6 olive, lime, and celery kabobs
- Wash down with 6 Bloody Marys (in which the above are immersed)

Lunch:
- 3 peanut butter and SPAM sandwiches
- 1 punch bowl of Kool-Aid spiked with grain alcohol

Dinner:
- *Viva Europe Carb Fest:* French toast, French fries, French bread, Spanish rice, English toffee, Swiss chocolate, and a Dutch baby

Supplement:
- 2 boxes pseudoephedrine

day four

MENU A

Breakfast:
- *I Love New York Breakfast Special:* Black coffee and cigarettes

Lunch:
- *Once, Twice, Three Times a Lunchmeat Sandwich:* 2 slices of Wonder bread with pimiento loaf, bologna, and pressed ham

Dinner:
- *Family Night:* Uncle Ben rice, Aunt Jemima pancakes, and Papa John's pizza

MENU B

Breakfast:
- *I Love New York Breakfast Special:* Black coffee and cigarettes

Lunch:
- Are you kidding? You ate two boxes of pseudoephedrine last night!

Dinner:
- Ditto

Supplement:
- 4 Ativan + 1 Red Bull with vodka. Good heavens, if you could only get some sleep.

 *retox recipes*

In an ideal world, we would either eat out or have dinner cooked for us every night. Or at least we'd be in a condition to hit the local corner store for some tasty snacks. Sadly, this is not always the case. For those instances when you find yourself stranded at home—whether you're too drunk, too high, too broke, or too not allowed to operate a motor vehicle—we've got some tantalizing recipes you can whip up from staples that have been languishing in your kitchen cupboard for years. Like the phoenix that rose from the proverbial ashes, masterpieces will arise from half-empty cupboards to see you through your hour of need.

MYSTERY BISQUE

Create an easy, hearty soup by grabbing five random cans out of your cupboard and mixing them together. Include some metal shavings and you'll get all the valuable nutrients found in cans, like heavy metals and lead. (Puffy cans are fortified with nutritious botulism!)

You will need:

5 cans of anything

1. Open all cans and dump into large saucepan.
2. Cook over medium-high heat until warm, about 5 minutes, stirring occasionally.

Serves 6

POOR MAN'S PANCAKES

Did you know that you don't *really* need milk and eggs to make pancakes? All it takes is a little know-how and positive thinking.

You will need:

2 cups pancake mix or reasonable substitute (e.g., cake mix, potato flakes, powdered sugar, cornstarch, or talc)

1$^1/_3$ cups milk or reasonable substitute (condensed milk, evaporated milk, or murky water)

1 egg or reasonable substitute (mayonnaise packets)

1 can fruit cocktail or reasonable substitute (jam, ketchup, or hard pellets from back of drawer that might be raisins)

1. In large mixing bowl, stir together pancake mix, milk, and egg (or reasonable substitutes) until smooth.

2. Pour by $^1/_4$ cupfuls into hot greased skillet. Cook until edges start to crisp. Flip and cook until golden.

3. Garnish with fruit topping.

Serves 4

MU SHU PIZZA

This miraculous dish combines all the unhealthiness of Chinese and
Italian cuisine in one convenient package. It's like a saturated-fat
summit meeting. Cheese and oil, together at last.

You will need:

1 phone
$16
1 carton leftover mu shu (or other Chinese
   food leftovers)
Soy sauce

1. Order large cheese pizza to be delivered to your home.
2. Heat leftover mu shu in microwave 3 to 4 minutes, or until mold no
longer smells.
3. Top pizza with mu shu. Douse liberally with soy sauce.

Serves 4

PIZZA IN A GLASS

This nutritious Bloody Mary variation is a meal and a drink in one!

You will need:

Ice

1 jar pizza sauce

1 fifth vodka, or however much you have left

String cheese

1. Fill tumbler with ice.

2. Scrape mold off sides of jar of pizza sauce.

3. Mix equal parts vodka and pizza sauce and pour in tumblers.

4. Peel mold off string cheese.

5. Stir drinks and serve. Garnish with string cheese swizzle sticks.

Serves 4

KOOL AID LATTE

Want a fancy fruity coffee drink but are in no condition to get to Starbucks? Whip up your own from ingredients you already have on hand! Make mine a venti.

You will need:

1 can sweetened condensed milk
Ice
1 packet Kool-Aid, any flavor
1 tablespoon warm water
4 crushed No-Doz tablets

1. Pour condensed milk over ice. Stir in Kool-Aid.

2. In small cup, stir together water and No-Doz. Add to milk mixture. Hoo! This stuff really wakes you up!

3. Clean kitchen floor with eyeshadow applicator, and then tweeze all the hair from arms.

Serves 1

DEEP FRIED TWINKIES

Your nephew's lunch supplies become a decadent dessert. You wouldn't think it would be possible to make a Twinkie tastier, but just try adding hot oil and frosting. Diabetes, here we come!

You will need:

8 Twinkies

Hot vegetable oil

1 tub frosting, any flavor

1. Drop Twinkies in deep-fat fryer, two at a time, for just a few seconds, until they are golden brown.

2. Let cool and top with ample amounts of frosting.

Serves 2

EXER-CISE

3

Stop pretending that you enjoy working out. No one enjoys working out. It's as boring as sleep, and not nearly as fun. It does nothing for your personality. Contrary to popular opinion, it actually makes you *less* attractive. Who wants to date someone whose hobby is lifting heavy objects? Who wants to forgo alcohol and cholesterol, and then go home early because you're "in training"? And Lycra? Please.

Go ahead and cancel your gym membership, because you're on the Retox program now. The idea is simple: you're already exercising more than you realize. Everything you do uses energy. Even eating burns calories. The trick is to take it just a little farther. Eat more, and burn more calories. And if you really want to push it, add some stimulants to the mix. It's like having Elvis as your personal trainer. Two boxes of cold medicine will get your heart rate up like you wouldn't believe. Try smoking next time you're on the treadmill. Feel the burn!

 *pill-ates*

In the last few years Pilates has become incredibly popular and damned if we know why. Have you tried it? It's really hard! The fact that Pilates was invented in Germany should tell you something. This is a rigorous practice meant for people who favor things like icy predawn swims at naturist camps and hiking boots for everyday wear. It's not for you.

It's certainly not for us. We prefer the fitness regime practiced by the slim and stylish citizens one country over. Have you ever noticed that there are no gyms in France, but there's a well-stocked pharmacy on every corner? Forget diets and exercise. Our French friends have proven that all you really need are pills, creams, and comestibles. Wash the pills down with some burgundy, and watch the kilos melt away!

Use the chart on pages 52-53 to match your current workout routine with its drugstore replacement.

IF YOU USED TO LIKE	TRY
Yoga	**Librium** Doing yoga burns 250 calories an hour. How is that relaxing? We say take a Librium instead. You'll get the blissed-out post-yoga glow without having to do a single downward-facing dog.
Triathlons	**Extra-strength decongestant + Red Bull + clove cigarettes** Competing in triathlons burns 700 calories an hour and you'll feel every one of them. Who needs it? A few tabs of nondrowsy decongestant, an energy drink, and a couple of bidis will crank your heart rate up to the same level and produce the same lung-burning effect in half the time. Way to go, iron man!
Pilates	**Ephedrine + cellulite-reducing cream + Rohypnol** Doing Pilates burns 300 calories an hour and reduces cellulite. So does eating a tab of ephedrine and slathering yourself in cellulite-reducing cream. OK, fine, that cellulite cream doesn't work *at all,* but if you add some Rohypnol to the mix you'll forget you have cellulite in the first place.

IF YOU USED TO LIKE	TRY . . .
	Weight Gainer 2200 Weight lifting burns 350 calories an hour. Weight Gainer 2200 *has* 2,200 calories a serving. We know the idea is to gain muscle, not just weight, but drinking a milkshake is a whole lot more pleasant than bench-pressing hundreds of pounds, so drink up. And man boobs sort of look like pecs, anyway. Bottoms up!
Weight Lifting	
	Lactaid Body sculpting burns 250 calories an hour. We're not sure how many Lactaid burns—we're just going on a hunch here—but if it can help your stomach break down cottage cheese, then maybe it can do the same for your thighs. Worth a try.
Body Sculpting	
	Drinking Swimming burns 600 calories an hour. If you chug until you throw up, drinking does too. And, like swimming, this activity involves a lot of liquid and can make the blood vessels in your eyes burst.
Swimming	

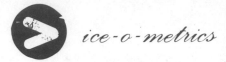 *ice-o-metrics*

If you hate the gym but love the gin, then have we got the workout plan for you. It turns out you're already burning loads of calories just by doing what you do best—knocking back a few cold ones. Drink your way to fitness with these easy, effective bar exercises.

The Beer Pint Bicep Curl

The most basic of all bar moves, this is ideal for both beginning drinkers and beginning exercisers. Simply place your elbow on the bar, grab your pint, and bring it to your mouth. Start with a light beer and gradually work your way up to heavier brews like stouts and porters. The key to

this one is lots of reps, so you'll want to keep it up until you move involuntarily to a more advanced exercise, like the Not-Quite-Empty Lunge or the Urinal Lean.

Calories burned: 75

The Sneaky Snacker Stretch

Sure, it's not sanitary, or even legal, to keep dipping your paws into the bar's supply of olives, cocktail onions, and cherries, but a person gets hungry, and besides, it's a good stretch. Simply wait until the bartender's back is turned, and reach. Good job!

Calories burned: 15

Calories consumed: 65

The Sloppy Drunk Purse Spill Toe Touch

It's so easy, after you've had a few, to accidentally dump the entire contents of your purse on the floor. Maybe you got clumsy while looking for a mint, or maybe you were trying to make a point while arguing with your jerky boyfriend. Whatever the reason all your shit ended up on the floor, it's an opportunity for an excellent stretch. Bend at the waist, reach down, and angrily shove everything back in your purse. Be sure to breathe, preferably loudly and huffily.

Calories burned: 20

The Not-Quite-Empty Lunge

Lunges are a great way to work large muscle groups. The next time that anal-retentive bartender starts clearing a drink you haven't quite finished, let her know in no uncertain terms that you don't plan to let go of it. Throw your whole body into it. Doesn't she look impressed now?

Calories burned: 20

Discarded Cigarette Butt Squat

You must be pretty loaded if you're on your hands and knees looking for cigarette butts that have been in other people's mouths before being stubbed out under their feet. Well, no sense beating yourself up over it, you need some nicotine and if this is how you have to get it, then so be it. Bend at the knees and squat down to see what you can find. Even if you don't come up with one, you'll know you just gave your own butt a good workout.

Calories burned: 35

Extremely Wasted Dancercise

Normally performed barefoot and alone, after you've lost your shoes. Where *are* your shoes, by the way? Maybe you left them in the bath-room. Well, screw it. This is your favorite song and you have to dance *right now*.

Calories burned: 200

Belligerent Drunk Kickboxing

Accuse someone of looking at you funny, then throw a drink in his face and wait for the fight to begin. Because you're more likely to hurt your-self than your opponent if you actually land any kicks or punches, it's good to be so inebriated that your aim is off. You'll get all the cardio benefits with none of the concussions.

Calories burned: 300

Drink and Dial Hamstring Stretch

This one's easy. Drink six beers and dial up an old boyfriend or girl-friend. Then grab your foot and stick it in your mouth.

Calories burned: 15

The Urinal Lean

You know you came in here to do something. What was it? Huh. Well, there's a urinal in front of you, your pants are unzipped, and there's this persistent pressure in the bladder region. Hmm. Still not ringing a bell. Sooo sleepy. What was it you were doing here again? While you try to remember what you came in here for, go ahead and lean your forearm and forehead against the wall and give your delts a nice stretch.

Calories burned: 15

Middle Finger Extensions

That guy at the end of the bar has been working your nerves all night and your middle finger is feeling a little cramped. Why don't you give it a little stretch in his direction?

Calories burned: 10

Morning-After Self-Kicks

If you actually remembered what you did last night, you'd probably want to work your lower body with a few kicks to the glutes. But you don't, and you won't, so pull the covers back over your head and sleep it off. Fitness is *hard*.

Calories burned: 30

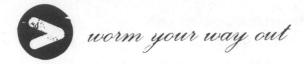 *worm your way out*

If you're like us, you want to be thinner but lack the willpower and motivation to stick with any diet for longer than twenty-four hours. You're torn: Look like a supermodel or eat that deep-fried taco on a stick? The pleasures of a sedentary lifestyle, or the heroin-chic glamour of an underaged Calvin Klein model? How to have it both ways, always? All you need to do to enjoy the fast food your little heart desires and never gain a pound is to host a parasite. To those people who say nothing worth having comes easy, we say, Ha! Meet your new best friend, the tapeworm.

Perhaps you've tried diets in the past. Or maybe you dabbled in diet pills or cocaine. Sure, there was a time when we all thought crystal meth was the new Crystal Light. Although all of these are viable weight-loss options, and they give you a mighty, mighty high, the sad truth is that the narcotic hangover is one tough mother. Yes, you'd be skinny as hell balled up on the bathroom floor, but no one would be there to see the leaner, meaner you. Try a parasite instead!

Sounds great! But is there a downside?

We're glad you asked. Some parasites and waterborne bacteria pack a lot of baggage. The hookworm, roundworm, and whipworm are among the leaders in intestinal subletters, but they tend to bring a whole army of pesky side effects that will distract people from complimenting you

on your new, lean bod (vomiting, diarrhea, stomach cramps, and so on). So choose your new belly buddy carefully.

Which parasite will work for me?

There sure are a lot of great bugs out there, but there's one little guy who really stands out. Our favorite guest to invite into our intestinal tracts is the tapeworm. He causes weight loss with few side effects, plus he's as easy to pick up as a dirty French whore.

I'm sold. Where can I find one of these weight-loss wonders?

Undercooked meat and fish are the gateway to the sleek, chic, new you. All you need to do is hit the taco truck and all-you-can-eat buffets as often as possible. Choose items that have been improperly heated in a steam table, like Swedish meatballs or chicken enchiladas Also, if there's a really long line at your favorite taqueria, chances are the cooks won't have the time or the wherewithal to cook your meat all the way. Undercooked pork is your best bet. Then, once you've got that parasite safely tucked away in your GI tract, you can chow down all you want and the pounds will melt away as your new "baby" takes one for the team.

yofa: staying limber the retox way

You've just settled onto the sofa with everything you need—remotes, a stash of snacks, and several forty-ouncers. Your goal: to spend twenty-four hours on the couch without getting up (except for potty runs). Your first few hours are smooth sailing. But when Mr. Kitty pushes your martini to the edge of the coffee table and you can't quite reach it, you realize how stiff you are—and what a liability that could be in your quest to break your couch camp-out record. Let's face it, drinking until four in the morning and then passing out on the kitchen floor has left your muscles in knots. You need Yofa, yoga you can do from the sofa. Practice these simple Yofa poses during commercial breaks and in no time you'll be as loose as a Jell-O shot.

The Angry Cat

On the couch, get on all fours and arch your back upward. Lift right arm and swat at imaginary fly. Repeat with left arm. Hissing is optional. Return to stationary position and reward self with doughnut.

The Downward Spiral

Sit Indian style on couch. Roll head clockwise until dizziness is achieved. Roll head counterclockwise until nausea is achieved. When equilibrium is regained, smoke menthol cigarette.

The Drunken Hobo

Sit upright on sofa with feet placed squarely on the floor. Lean as far as you can to the right without falling over. Correct self and lean as far to the left as possible. Repeat, leaning forward and backward as well. Repeat set four times or until the commercials are over.

The Fiery Bowel

Lie on couch with back flat and knees up. Place arms over tummy. Slowly twist head to the left and groan. Slowly twist head to the right and groan. Repeat until lower GI distress (real or imagined) has abated. Eat bag of jalapeño potato chips, wait for abdominal distress, and repeat.

The Lord of the Dance Pose

Lie flat on couch and fold arms over chest. Bring left knee up and kick leg up and down several times. Repeat with right leg. Continue until roommates start to make fun of you. Reward self with shot of Irish whiskey. Headband is optional.

The Flatulent Dog

Lie on left side in fetal position. Lift right leg up, and hold position for thirty seconds. Switch sides and repeat with left leg. Displays of actual flatulence are optional.

YOFA SUPPLIES

Yoga requires all kinds of accessories, like sticky mats and something called a bolster. We think you'll agree that Yofa supplies are much tastier:

1 box Entenmann's cookies
1 bag Funyuns
1 bag salt and vinegar chips
1 box powdered mini doughnuts
1 box red wine (white needs to be chilled, which requires getting up)
1 bottle whiskey
1 jar maraschino cherries
1 martini shaker
1 martini glass
1 bottle pills of your choice
3 magazines
1 whistle to alert roommates that you need something
1 universal remote control

BEFORE

AFTER

GROOM -ING

4

Sure, change begins on the inside, but that doesn't mean you have to go around looking like a loser. Clear skin and healthy hair advertise to the world you're a wet blanket. Obviously, you're spending your nights at home steaming your pores and taking your vitamins. A date with you would probably involve organic food, a nature hike, and a self-righteous lecture about recycling. Boring! What you want is a look that says, "I've been around the block and I'm looking forward to another loop." Get ready for a Retox makeover. These beauty tips will transform you from a mousy do-gooder to a flashy good time. They'll also help you camouflage the dents and dings that come with the twenty-four-hour party lifestyle. Best of all, they'll free you from the PC concerns that have kept you frizzy and flaky since college. Ozone-destroying hair spray? Yes, please! Moisturizer tested on baby bunnies? Why not? You're worth it!

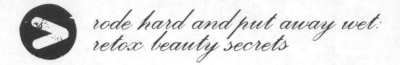

rode hard and put away wet: retox beauty secrets

It's sad but true: lack of sleep, gallons of alcohol, and loads of fried foods can take their toll. Dim light and beer goggles can hide only so much. But that's no reason to return to healthy living! Instead, try these quick-fix ideas. They'll help you conceal the under-eye circles, cold sores, and other blemishes that come with the Retox lifestyle.

Puffy Eyes

Sometimes after a night of heavy drinking, light sleeping, or passive-aggressive crying, you wake up with swollen, puffy eyes. The Retox fix? Preparation H. Apply liberally around eyes and watch them deflate. While you're at it, try applying some on your butt and thighs and see if they don't get less swollen, too.

Missing Eyebrow

Have you ever woken up with one eyebrow missing? Of course you have—you're human. The Retox fix? Shave off the remaining eyebrow and start from scratch. You can pencil them in if you want, but we think it's much more fun to glue on a fake mustache instead. Get a variety pack at the costume shop and go to town. Change your look depending on your mood du jour.

Frizzy Hair

When your hair puffs up like a giant Brillo pad and there's no time to waste, simply apply ½ teaspoon of vegetable oil and watch the flyaways land. No vegetable oil on hand? Just rub hair with a Tater Tot. (For longer hair, use french fries.)

Greasy Hair

Perhaps you used ½ cup vegetable oil instead of ½ teaspoon when trying to defrizz your hair, or maybe you're just European. Either way, if you have greasy hair, we have the fix. Apply 1 tablespoon of cake mix to the roots of your hair and work through. The flour will absorb the oil, and you'll smell like a Twinkie!

Blemishes

Welcome to Retox Color Theory 101. Any skin discoloration can be neutralized by applying the opposite color on the color wheel and then covering with concealer. Got a red zit? Apply green as your basecoat. Blue bags under your eyes? Neutralize with orange. Yellow nicotine stains around the mouth? Dab with purple. Black permanent marker on your forehead labeling you "Bitch Boy"? Oof—can't help you there. Next time try not to pass out on the frat couch, 'K?

The Big Ones

And then there are the things that can't be so easily disguised. Black eyes, cold sores, spontaneous unexplained bald patches—these things happen. Fortunately, there's always the costume shop. Eye patches, false mustaches, and wigs will help you conceal the big flaws and have fun at the same time. Everyone likes an accessory. You may find yourself still using that neck brace long after the hickey has gone away.

the pretty mess makeover

Some people work for hours trying to achieve that "I'm not trying at all" look. That "I just got out of bed" look. That "I just took a handful of barbiturates and gave my boss a lap dance" look. And it's a good look, but the thing is, these messy celebrities we emulate aren't going for a certain look, they're just being themselves. Here's how you can be them, too.

Rock Star on the Skids

Begin by having several cocktails, and follow with a few pills of your choice. Then start making decisions about your look. Is a bra an appropriate replacement for a shirt? Yes, it is. Does your lipstick look better on your lips or all around your mouth? All around your mouth, of course. Feeling sleepy? Why not take a little nap and get your hair good and matted?

Bad-Boy Actor

The key to obtaining the bad-boy look is to smoke while you do everything. When you get dressed, fix your hair, or do any other forms of primping, you must have a cigarette in your hand or mouth at all times. Keep showering to a minimum. Replace hygiene with nicotine.

Skanky Starlet

Begin by doing all your shopping in the juniors department, always buying a size too small. On second thought, why not just shop in the children's department? Or, better yet, the infant's? Nothing is sexier than an actual baby tee. And remember, the lower the pants, the lovelier the thong. Don't forget to get your belly button pierced.

Former Child Star

The hottest look for former child stars these days is the prison jump-suit. Sadly, these aren't available retail, so you'll have to earn one for yourself. Tried-and-true former-child-star methods of obtaining these kicky little numbers include robbing a convenience store, carrying ille-gal drugs in one's car, and attempting manslaughter.

Diva with a Drinking Problem

The Retox lifestyle in no way supports drinking and driving. Frankly, we don't support driving at all—that's what friends and significant others are for. Instead, just pretend. Sit on the toilet with your makeup case and start swerving around. Now try to put all your makeup on and get dressed while you veer back and forth, left and right. That's *Miss* Diva with a Drinking Problem to you!

 *hundred-proof home spa*

The word *spa* actually comes from the Belgian term for "watering place." So why not model your home spa on your favorite watering hole? That's right, why not make your beauty treatments from alcohol? It makes other people look great—you down five or six cocktails, and everyone looks like a ten. You can look like one too, with these boozy beauty treatments.

You're Soaking in It: The Five-Martini Manicure

Remember how relaxed Madge got soaking her hands in Palmolive? Well, imagine how much more relaxed she'd have been if she were soaking herself in gin! Simply make and drink five martinis. Save the olives, remove the pimiento center, and place on fingertips. Pretty!

Margarita Facial

If rubbing alcohol shrinks your pores, then, contrary to all evidence, *drinking* alcohol might, too, right? Let's find out. Dunk head in a trough of margaritas. Can you feel it working? No? Try drinking it instead. *Uno mas,* for good measure. Some people think tequila has psychoactive properties. Can you feel your pores getting smaller? You can totally feel them *shrinking*, can't you? What's in this stuff? Can you hear the lime juice? You must be on some astral journey. It's like the music has color, and you're part of the music, and you're turning different colors. This stuff is fabulous. Wow wow wow your pores are so small. You are the lizard king. Li! Zard! King!

Bottle Massage

Sure, hot stones are nice, but they're not nearly as relaxing as a whole lot of beer. Drink a twelve-pack. Flail around incoherently as you lie on top of the empties, and then pass out. You'll wake up to blissfully tenderized muscles. As for the pounding headache, try massaging your head from the inside with another forty ounces of liquid muscle relaxant.

Hot Toddy Steam Treatment

Steaming your face opens pores and lets the impurities out. You could just use hot water, but wouldn't a hot toddy be much more fun? Heat up a mixture of whiskey, lemon juice, and honey in a mixing bowl. A mug is just too small, and it's not like you're going to drink it, at least not *all* of it. Lean your face over the bowl and cover your head with a towel tent. Mmm. Soooothing. Feel all those impurities leaving. Hey, you know where else you probably have impurities? Your stomach. Maybe you should drink some of the toddy after all. That would probably kill them off. Mmm. That's pretty good. You know what? You might as well finish it. You're out of plastic wrap, and it wouldn't keep anyway.

Conditioning Beer Rinse

In the 1970s, for some reason it became popular to wash your hair with beer. In our opinion all this accomplished was to waste a lot of beer. You've seen '70s hair. It didn't look good. Apparently, when hair gets drunk, it becomes dry and frizzy. It is, however, really fun to bring beer into the shower with you. Try this treatment instead: Douse hair with normal conditioner. Leave in as long as it takes to down a beer. Rinse. Repeat.

A Good Wallow: The Retox Bath

If essential oils and dried flowers don't soothe you, then maybe booze and tobacco will. You could infuse the water with them, but it would probably be more effective just to infuse yourself. So go ahead and climb in for a bathtime three-way with Jim Beam and Phillip Morris. Take me away.

 *jbf hairdos*

Just-been-f---ed hair is nothing to be ashamed of. It's a badge of honor, and it's not just for the promiscuous. Maybe you got your hair all messed up driving around in a convertible. Or maybe you've just had a lot going on—what with the bench warrant and the IRS trouble, who would have time to comb it every day? Well, don't you worry your nitty little head. We've got lots of suggestions to whip that JBF mess into a dynamic 'do. Try one of these great looks:

The Royal Mess
Favored by strung-out rock stars and easy prom queens alike, this hair-do couldn't be simpler. Just crown your freshly napped-on hair with a tiara. That's *Queen* Skank to you!

The Rico Suave
JBF hair for him. This *muy macho* hairstyle says, "I do whatever I want—and I will do it again, señor." Just cover with a bandana or do-rag. *Que guapo!*

Keep on Truckin'
Popular with starlets making the walk of shame home after a big night out. Don't worry about trying to drag a comb through that mess—you'll

just end up damaging your extensions. Instead, hide the whole thing under a trucker hat. Add big sunglasses and some thong-exposing low-rise Juicy sweats, and you'll be sure to make the cover of next week's *Us*!

The Re-Hive

No hairstyle is better suited for sleeping on than the pillowy beehive. A favorite of 1960s mistresses, it's basically JBF hair to begin with, all molded into a cone and held fast with hair spray. If it actually gets dislodged (unlikely), just tuck it back in place and secure with hairpins (if at a motel) or staples (at the office).

The Happy Hippie

Free love may be great for your soul, but it's hard on your hair, man. All that futon-hopping can make for some serious tangles. Well, don't let it harsh your mellow. Just mat the mess down with a little patchouli oil and tie a headband around your forehead. Combed-out hair is for *squares*.

The JBFro

Pity the naturally curly. When JBFed, their locks do not mat; they stand up and riot. It's like wearing a big flashing sign on your head that says, "I didn't make it home last night." It also says, "I've given up on grooming" and "I'm a crazy person." Sure, you could try to pick it out, but what are

the chances that you have a comb on you? You don't even know where your *underwear* is. Just run on home.

JBF Back to the '80s

You don't choose this style—it chooses you. If your orchestral maneuvers in the dark have left you with an asymmetrical mess—matted on one side, and ratted on the other—then there's nothing to do but go Cure on it. Douse the whole thing in black spray paint. Accessorize with eyeliner, smeared lipstick, and ennui. And, of course, lots of black rubber bracelets.

RELAX-ATION

5

Doesn't it seem like relaxation has become a lot of work? Running from yoga class to crystal therapy, trying to squeeze in thirty minutes of chanting before your acupressure appointment—who has the time? That's why our mantra is "It's time for my meds, nursey." These Retox relaxation techniques will have you loosey-goosey in the time that it takes to metabolize an opiate—twenty minutes on an empty stomach, or just one if you've got push-button morphine connections. Nirvana, baby.

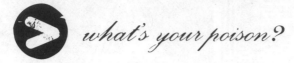 *what's your poison?*

So you're on your way to a life of drug or alcohol abuse. Congratulations! We think you'll enjoy your relaxing new lifestyle. But before you leap in with both kidneys, you'll want to find the intoxicant that suits you best. Are you a pill popper or a boozehound at heart? Do you have a soft spot for inhalants, or are you more of an over-the-counter type? Take our easy quiz to find the substance that's right for you.

1. When stressed, I:
   a. go for a run
   b. take a soothing bath
   c. drink a bottle of Nyquil

2. My idea of fun is:
   a. mountain biking
   b. a day at the spa
   c. shopping for Nyquil

3. I can't live without my:
   a. Tae Bo class
   b. sleep mask
   c. Nyquil

4. Friends describe me as:

   a. energetic

   b. mellow

   c. Nyquilly

5. My dream vacation is:

   a. cross-country skiing

   b. lying on the beach

   c. drinking Nyquil until I pass out

6. My pet peeve is:

   a. shin splints

   b. getting up early

   c. running out of Nyquil

Key

Mostly As: You enjoy a natural high. Well, wait until you try an *unnatural* one! Stimulant abuse is the life for you. No-Doz, diet pills, Dexedrine—you'll enjoy them all. You'll finally have the energy to finish those projects you've been dying to get to, like cleaning every square inch of your house with a toothbrush while grinding your molars down to stubs. Go get 'em, Tiger!

Mostly Bs: You're easy like Sunday morning. Booze or barbiturates—it's your choice. Either one will complement your mellow-yellow lifestyle. Using both at once might put you in a coma, but you wouldn't really mind that, would you, Sleepy Jean?

Mostly Cs: You'd make a great Nyquil addict. In fact, you probably already are one. You haven't had a sore throat or a bad night's sleep in years. Of course, if you go more than a few hours without the stuff, you get the shakes like you wouldn't believe, but happily, there's a cure for that—more Nyquil!

HIGH MAINTENANCE

Remember, substance abuse is a marathon, not a sprint. You'll need to build endurance and stamina. We're here to help you do just that with tips to keep that hard-earned buzz going. When you wake up drunk the next day, you'll know you've succeeded.

Food

Food is the hard partyer's best friend and worst enemy. You want enough food in your stomach to keep you from passing out early (the pros calling this "getting your base on"). But too much might keep you from getting wasted in the first place. Play it safe and stick to foods that encourage even more drinking, like chips and salsa, or buffalo wings.

Rest

You need to give you body time to rest and recover. 8:00 to 10:00 P.M. is ideal. Known as the "disco nap," this little respite will ensure that you have the energy to keep going until closing and beyond.

Water

It's important to stay hydrated. Water will keep you from getting too drunk or too high too fast. It will also leave you equipped to urinate on someone's car, should circumstances require it.

the bait and switch massage

Besides a fistful of Valium, there's nothing more relaxing than getting a massage. And there's nothing less relaxing than giving one. The hand cramps, the uncomfortable squatting—who needs it? You can't even enjoy your own rubdown because of the nagging thought that you'll have to return the favor. It's time to end the tyranny of the "you do me, I'll do you" crap. Try these tricks to ensure that this two-way street becomes a one-lane road leading straight to you and your needs.

The Sore Hand Hoax

Start with the traditional "let's trade massages" maneuver, and make sure you get yours first. When you sense that the massage is winding down, ask your massager to work on your hands because they are really sore due to remote control carpal tunnel, martini mixing gone bad, or other repetitive motions. As your hands are getting rubbed, scream out in pain. Try yelling, "Are you trying to crush my bones?" Accuse your massager of not knowing her own strength, but encourage her to try again on the other hand. Repeat moaning and screaming. Wrap up by explaining that you had wanted to return the favor, but seeing how your hands are now just crumpled masses of broken bones and skin you no longer think it will be possible. Cap with promises not to press assault charges so you look like the good guy.

The Sleepy Angel

Again, start with the "you do me, I'll do you" massage ruse. Throughout the massage, say how great it is, how relaxed you feel. Then play dead.

When your massager tells you it's over and it's his turn now, start snoring. If he has the nerve to try to wake you up, explode with smarting remarks such as "I can't believe you woke me up when you know I have to get up at five in the morning to feed the homeless" and "I guess the insomnia that has plagued me my entire life means less to you than your own petty needs." Get worn out by the tirade, roll over, and resume playing dead.

The Emergency Phone Call

This one requires some advance planning and good timing, so it should only be used if you've already exhausted your other massage schemes. Ask a friend to call you at, say, 11:00 P.M., faking an emergency. Then ask your partner if she wants to swap massages at 10:30. Get your massage, and then, right when it's time for you to return the favor, the phone will ring and you'll get called away. Be sure to loudly say things like "She did *what* to you?" and "Don't worry, sad lost soul, I'm not going anywhere" until your partner gives up and goes to bed.

The Good-Gracious, You're-Contagious Scam

Get things going in the usual manner. Make sure that your massage partner takes off his shirt when it's time for you to deliver on your promise. Before you start, pretend to notice something on his back. Ask him if he's ever had bouts of ringworm before. Tell him you see several small circles on his back, and you're quite sure it's ringworm. If he tries to deny that he's contaminated and contagious, say that you're pretty sure ringworm comes from poor bathroom hygiene to shame him into submission. Tell him that when he learns how to wipe properly and that dirty worm problem clears up, you'll be happy to give him a massage.

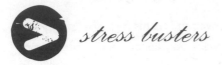 *stress busters*

Everyone's on the go these days. For some, it's go to tai chi class, go to the farmers' market, go to the acupuncturist, go to the vitamin store. For others, it's go to the bar, go to the pharmacy, go to the black-market pharmacy, go to the parole officer's. Either way, you're on the run. You're stressed and you need to calm down. You need a relaxing hobby. Try one of these!

Journaling

We know how it is: you're overworked and underpaid. The boss is breathing down your neck, cracking the corporate whip. He's already woken you up once (thereby putting the kibosh on your original de-stressing plan) and you need to get away from the grind without leaving the office. It's time for a potty break. Sneak off to the bathroom with a black marker. Inscribe the stall with a stream of obscenities that would make a sailor blush. Some people call it vandalism. We call it therapy. When you return to your desk, you'll feel clearheaded and refreshed, having relieved more than your bladder during your bathroom break.

Driving

How about a relaxing drive? Choose a pretty route with plenty of scenery and green trees. Still feeling grumpy? Maybe you wouldn't if other people knew how to drive. Start honking and giving people the finger. What is wrong with everyone? Why isn't the car in front of you moving? Maybe they're asleep and you need to rouse them by gently

Golf

Sometimes even your home can feel like a prison. It's dirty and cluttered, loud and chaotic. You need to escape into the great outdoors. Golf is a great stress buster because, while it's technically a sport, you're encouraged to drink, smoke, and drive while you play. Hit the green and take a few swings. Not feeling better yet? Try swinging at the golf cart instead. Go for the tires—they can take a beating. Still feeling stressed? How about that cute little squirrel? He may look harmless, but he's mocking your golf skills and should be punished. Run after the squirrel with your nine iron. Swing at everything that gets in your way. Soon you'll feel light as a feather.

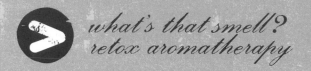

what's that smell?
retox aromatherapy

Some people call it huffing. We call it therapy! The right scent can truly turn your mood around. Try sniffing these mood-altering substances:

For serenity: We don't know about you, but nothing soothes us like the smell of gasoline. Sometimes, when we're getting a fill-up, we become so serene we wake up with our head on the horn.

For energy: We bet you'll really enjoy the smell of your nephew's ground-up Ritalin tablets. Wow, does the scent get you going! You'll be in rehab before you know what hit you!

For joy: Try aerosol computer cleaner. For some reason, knowing you have a really clean computer makes you feel super joyous, especially if you're working in a room with poor ventilation.

For bliss: Sniff a really great chardonnay. What a fine bouquet that has! Really get in there; don't be shy. Did your nose just touch the wine? It sure did. No one else will want it now, so you might as well drink it. Mmm. Bliss.

For insight: There's nothing like the smell of the coffee to wake you up to the twenty-four-hour shit party that is your life. Insight sucks. You know what might help, though? *Irish* coffee. The delicious boozy smell (and boozy booze) will have you feeling wise in no time.

For contentment: Cookies! You can't breathe them, but you sure can inhale them. Try eating a whole package of Chips Ahoy in half an hour. You'll feel so contented you'll spend the rest of the afternoon contentedly on the couch, clutching your belly and moaning with the painful bloat of satisfaction.

For levity: Whip-it cartridges turn heavy cream into a light-as-a-feather dessert topping. They can do the same to your brain! Lighten your load with a whiff of their delightful scent. Wait. What were we just talking about? Whipped cream is yummy!

For creativity: The smell of spray paint really inspires artistic expression, especially if you forget to wear your safety mask.

For productivity: When you're lagging at work, nothing gets you going again like the smell of whiteout. You'll be amazed at how much you can get done. Sure, that report might not make all that much sense, and it may be full of mistakes, but that will just give you the opportunity to use even more whiteout, making you even more productive. It's brilliant! You should patent this idea! Dammit, why aren't you the boss?

For discretion: It's really no one's business what you do on your lunch hour, is it? And if you want to spend it in a gin-soaked haze at a topless bar, you should be able to without anyone saying, "You smell like stripper," or "Geez, Phil, did you fall into a distillery?" A little Bengay can help you do just that. It will overpower any other scents you may have picked up and make people think you spent your lunch hour at the gym. And the sharp smell of menthol will instantly transform your mood from guilty to virtuous, and isn't transforming your mood what aromatherapy is all about?

RELATION 6 -SHIPS

Maybe you think you've found the love of your life. Or maybe you already know that the person you wake up to every day is a four-star loser. Either way, at some point, you are going to want to kill him or her and you'll need some relationship help to see you through. Let us save you a little time. Men are from Mars, women are from Venus, crap is from Uranus, and that's exactly what 99 percent of relationship books are. Worst of all are the ones that actually work. The *last* thing you and your partner want is to communicate more effectively. If each of you actually knew what the other truly thought, you'd kill yourselves. Dr. Phil will tell it like it is, but that's just asking for trouble. If you admit how bad things are, you'll probably have to break up, and even a miserable lifetime shackled to a raving lunatic is better than being alone with your own terrifying neediness for five seconds. So skip the how-to books, cancel the couples counseling, and rely on the tried-and-true Retox relationship techniques instead. They'll work on your partner, your best friend, your family, or anyone with whom you've been trading resentments for years. A highly effective combination of self-medication, passive-aggressive manipulation, shame, and guilt, they're guaranteed to keep you and your loved ones locked in the same destructive patterns for the rest of your life. And if that's not love, what is?

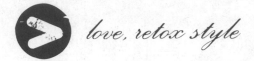
love, retox style

Some say there is no greater force on earth than love, and we agree. What else could make you leave fifty messages on someone's answering machine, steal his password and check his e-mail, then stand outside in the pouring rain just to make sure he's OK because a catastrophic accident is surely the only reason he hasn't called you back? It's love, baby, and it makes the world go round. Here are the phases to expect in a Retox relationship.

Say My Name, Bitch

The initial stages of love are both blissful and bewildering. There are passionate kisses and awkward moments. And nothing's more awkward than realizing you've been sleeping with someone for three weeks and you don't even know his last name. Not to worry, you just need to get your hands on his ID. This can be done several ways. Assuming that you'll be spending most of your quality time at the bar, simply ask to see his ID after the bartender does. If he's a little too "seasoned" to be carded, ask to see his AARP card. When all else fails, go for his wallet when he gets out of bed to pee.

Love Me, Love My Hangover

The next stage of love is when the reality begins to set in. The honeymoon is over, and we start to see the flaws in our partners. While it's fine for you to criticize your mate, it's important to establish from the get-go that you come *as is*—no refunds or exchanges. Here are some

handy phrases to help reinforce this notion:

"But I thought that was one of the things you loved about me."

"I was like this when we first started dating."

"If you really loved me, you'd love *all* of me."

"When I pass out on the bathroom floor, I'm telling you how comfortable I am with you."

You Call It Co-dependency, We Call It Co-mmitment

As your relationship matures and progresses, it will move toward a total merger of two lives—to the point where your problems and your mate's are indistinguishable. There are many perks that come with this level of intimacy. While it's true that we promote the me, me, me approach to life, there are times when it's best to have the spotlight off of you—for instance, during a crime investigation, or when focusing on personal problems and emotional shortcomings. If you're all wrapped up in your partner's problems you won't have any time to focus on your own. Besides that, it's just plain fun. With all of the drama that comes with a stormy relationship, there is always cause to drink, smoke, and self-medicate just to make it through the constant emotional chaos. And as an extra added bonus, you'll probably drop a few pounds because you'll frequently be too upset to eat.

passive aggression: make loving fun

There's no shortage of relationship guides out there, and if they worked you'd be happy already, wouldn't you? Some of them advise you not to return calls; others, to answer the door wearing nothing but plastic wrap. Forget all that. The only thing that works is passive aggression. Your unpredictable mood swings will keep your relationship fresh, and your saccharine sarcasm will ensure your partner never strays. Stick to the following tried-and-true passive-aggressive relationship tips.

Tip #1: Ride the Snake

Nothing keeps a relationship exciting like an emotional roller coaster. Why say it when you can spit it? Why not break down in tears at the dinner table? Swing those moods and soon you'll be swinging from the chandeliers, too. Sexy!

Tip #2: Come Closer/Go Away

This is a super-fun game that both you and your partner will love. To play, simply pull away at every turn. Flinch at her touch and respond to questions with curt one-word answers. When she starts giving you the space you're clearly asking for, act hurt and needy. When she responds with affection, start all over again.

Tip #3: Sarcasm—*Nice* Technique

Experts say that most relationship problems are caused by communication breakdowns. Sometimes it's hard for your partner to know what you really mean by "I'm pregnant, and I'm not kidding" or "Dating you was the biggest mistake of my life." Why not simplify things by getting rid of sincerity entirely? Say everything in a sarcastic tone and your partner will know exactly where he stands. And when it's your turn to listen, let him know you're actively listening by rolling your eyes all the way back.

Tip #4: Go Sybil

If a blonde wig can make a person feel like he has a whole new partner, imagine what a psychotic alter ego will do! It's like dating twins! One twin brings you breakfast in bed, while the other one slashes your tires. Sometimes you're passive, sometimes straight-up aggressive. Who will you be today?

Tip #5: I'm Rubber, You're Glue

Psychologists call this "projection," and it's a handy technique. Explain it to your partner this way: everything you accuse me of, you actually are yourself. Your mate will never call you a cheap-ass ho bag again!

BACKHANDED COMPLIMENTS

Nothing undermines self-esteem like the backhanded compliment. Administered daily, these passive-aggressive emotional missiles will keep loved ones faithful for fear they'll never find someone else. Try these surefire lines:

"I don't care what my sister says, those shorts don't make your ass look huge *at all.*"

"You got into college with a 950 SAT score? Wow. You must be really good with people, or something."

"Most people with your short waist couldn't get away with a fitted pullover, but you kind of make it work somehow."

"I like those shoes. They make your feet look much smaller."

"What? I said it's a very *ladylike* mustache."

"That festering pimple on your chin is *barely* noticeable."

"I've never met a girl who could eat as much as you do."

"Honey, you know I find thinning hair attractive."

"You hold your liquor even better than your mother does!"

"Not everyone can be successful."

"I love you even if you'll never amount to anything."

better loving through chemistry

Sure, couples therapy might work sometimes, but medication is a million times faster and cheaper. So cancel your appointment with Dr. Touchyfeely and call Dr. Feelgood instead. Here are our prescriptions for these common relationship challenges:

Moving in Together

It goes without saying that you'll both be going on an antidepressant. The pleasant side effect of a decreased libido will leave you that much more time to accomplish the really important things, like accidentally giving his LP collection to Goodwill or undermining her self-esteem with a daily volley of veiled criticism.

Getting Engaged

Warm those feet up with a toasty sedative habit. It'll help you forget your nagging worries about your fiancé's anger management problems and unresolved intimacy issues so you can focus on your priorities, like getting married before your younger sibling.

The Wedding

If ever there were a marriage made in heaven, it's SSRIs and alcohol. If you've drunk two glasses of chardonnay while taking an antidepressant and woken up in the wreckage of your former car after a six-hour blackout, then you know there's nothing like this combo to get you through stressful times. The cake collapsed? The band didn't show? The pastor doesn't know your name? Who cares? You'll never remember any of it if you toast your union with the one-two punch of cheap reception champagne and prescription meds. (Recommended only if your new spouse comes with fabulous medical, car, and life insurance.)

Visiting the In-Laws

Go immediately to DEFCON 5. If there's a situation that calls for intravenous assistance, this is it. But no one wants to nod out in the soup course. Instead, why not turn to the coward's heroin: hard-core pain meds. Oxycontin, Fentanyl, push-button morphine—you're entitled. Because, really, after the third time your mother-in-law has made a dig about your hair, are you in any less pain than an accident victim?

Family Planning

Sadly, fertility concerns mean you'll have to replace the drugs you actually enjoy with ones that make you psychotically moody. No opiates, no caffeine—you can't even have *soft cheeses*. Come *on*! Which is why we recommend you rethink the no-booze policy. There's some evidence that fetal alcohol syndrome is a myth, and, even if it's not, it keeps the birth weight down for an easier delivery! Besides, if you don't get a damn brandy Alexander soon this baby will probably never even get conceived in the first place. So go ahead and knock a couple back. Remember, you're drinking for two!

 *good-bye and good riddance*

Sometimes, sadly, even manipulation doesn't work, and you have to say good-bye. One of the hardest parts of a comprehensive life-changing regime like Retox is letting go of friends and family who won't help you work your new program. This list may include, but is not limited to, your yoga instructor, nutritionist, therapist, life coach, and all your do-gooder friends. We know it's hard. Actually, come to think of it, it's not *that* hard—these people are self-righteous jackasses. Here's our handy three-step plan to lose the losers:

Phase 1: Apathy

First, stop returning phone calls. A lot of these "friends" are just in it for their own martyrdom, not because they actually care about you. Phase 1 is also a good time to stop showering. This will eliminate stink-fearing pansies (it will, however, leave the hippies hanging around, but we'll get to them later).

Phase 2: Lying

Lying is something we all do every day, whether we like to admit it or not. "Yes, your homemade soy-nut carrot cake is delicious." "Yes, I listen to NPR all the time, too." "No, I did not steal your watch." Phase 2 is just taking it one step further. Below are some handy lies that will send people packing:

"I have a highly contagious strain of hepatitis C and I have to be quarantined for six months."

"I'm moving to the West Indies."

"I think I saw your spouse and his/her secretary kissing."

"I'm gay and I don't think you support my new lifestyle so we can't be friends." (Substitute "straight" for "gay" if you really are gay.)

"I've joined the army."

"I've joined Amway."

Phase 3: Action

For those hangers-on who just won't take the hint (we're talking to you, hippies), drastic action is necessary—acts of unforgivable treason. Here's a list of sins that will get rid of even the most noble (and clueless) of your friends and family:

Crash their car.

Cut their hair while they're sleeping.

Show up at their workplace drunk and naked.

Give their children alcohol and cigarettes.

Join Amway.

SELF-DEVELOPMENT

So, the self-improvement is going pretty well, isn't it? You've been in therapy for years, and now you're so neurotic that you spend your sessions discussing how it makes you feel *when the receptionist forgets to say hello*. The motivational seminar that was supposed to Awaken the Giant Within just put the troll without to sleep. And the only way the self-help books have changed your life is that now you no longer have room on your bookshelves for the books you actually want to read, like those by Jackie Collins. In short, you've spent a fortune on self-development and all it's done is make you self-absorbed. Maybe it's time to stop trying to better yourself and develop your weak points instead. Greed can be an *asset*. Denial can *save your life*. Our self-development tips will show you how to make narcissism work for you. Demoralize your friends? Destroy your coworkers? Take what you want from the rubble of their shattered lives? Yes, you can!

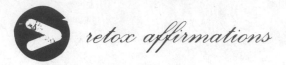 *retox affirmations*

If therapy, empowerment training, and astrology have failed to improve your life, it may be time for you to try affirmations. Repeated daily, these powerful statements can effect real change. Motivational speakers and recurring *Saturday Night Live* characters know: affirmations work. Try repeating these affirmations and see if they don't start working for you.

"I will not have more than four drinks tonight."

"OK, I will have five drinks, but I will not have six."

"I will not beat myself up for having six drinks."

"I can have six drinks and behave perfectly appropriately."

"I will not take my pants off in public."

"I am a free spirit."

"I am a free spirit who cannot be bound by society's bogus dress code."

"I work hard and deserve to relax every once in a while, what with the boss breathing down my neck all the time and the ball and chain riding my ass night and day."

"I will not eat a stranger's buffalo wings when he gets up to go to the bathroom."

"I am a deserving person who is open to the generosity of the universe."

"I am a fun drunk."

"I am a fun drunk who, OK, gets a little moody but I think we can all agree that I have plenty to be moody about."

"I will not decide it's a good idea to call my partner and give her a piece of my mind."

"I will not decide it's a good idea to vent my rage on the condom dispenser, then fall asleep in a bathroom stall."

"I am a thoughtful person who is open to suggestions, except for the suggestion that I leave and never come back."

"I will not throw up in the cab." "I will not suggest to the cab driver that it is he, and not the puddle of half-digested buffalo wings on the upholstery, that smells like vomit."

"I won't ever let this happen again."

"I will not lie to myself."

denial: the new self-esteem

In the 1950s, America was made up of contentedly ignorant families who happily changed the subject when an unsavory topic was broached. Wives would turn a blind eye to the lipstick on their husband's collars, husbands would pretend not to notice the empty bottles of vodka spilling from the garbage, and they would both accept their children's claims that that odd contraption was for burning incense. That was how people got by, and they were *happy*. Then some hippie-ass therapist decided this was not OK and we needed to wake up and smell the patchouli. Families were torn apart, people were left alone to face their problems and shortcomings, and everyone was miserable. We think it's time to return to a simpler era when serious discussion was off-limits and ignorance reigned supreme. You call it denial. We like to think of it as optimism.

Do-gooder types are always touting the power of positive thinking. But what about the power of not thinking at all? This is an equally useful tool that will help you get through the day. Will worrying about your police record make it go away? No! Will wondering if your liver is functioning make it any healthier? No! Will *not* thinking about these things make you feel better? You betcha!

Is your glass half full or half empty? If it's half empty, it's time to top it off with some more whiskey! Just think how rosy the world will look then. Let's practice right now. Look at the pictures on pages 114–16 and learn to see them as we do:

a. Mommy's a drunk.

b. Mommy's always happy.

a. Money-eating machine

b. Long-term investment plan

a. Person engaging in violence

b. Person giving voice to her feelings

a. My boyfriend is gay.

b. My boyfriend is sensitive, well-dressed, and enjoys antiquing with me.

a. Shoplifting

b. Protesting corporate America

a. Drank till he puked

b. Getting some well-deserved rest

a. Kimmy's headed for juvy.

b. Kimmy's found a new hobby.

Choose B. Choose denial. Choose life. *L'chaim!*

HOW TO MANIPULATE YOUR THERAPIST

Contrary to what you might think, therapy can work well with the Retox regime. Remember—your shrink is a direct line to obtaining drugs legally. And, just as important, your therapist is a captive audience for the one-man freak show that is your life. Every time you enter that office you're walking on stage and you're the star. Remember that you are in charge and it's your job to keep your therapist under your thumb. Let her know who's the boss with some manipulative behavior strategies.

The best way to do this is by constantly changing your behavior patterns. Find that Abnormal Psych textbook from your brief stint in college, choose a disorder, and pretend to have it for a few weeks. When you see your doctor gaining confidence, switch to an entirely different disorder to keep her on her toes. The benefit of this is twofold: it provides endless amounts of entertainment while at the same time making her feel insecure and inept.

It's very important, before you begin therapy, to select the doctor who's right for you—and by that we mean a doctor who plays fast and loose with her prescription pad. If that doesn't work, you should consider stealing it. Ask a friend to phone in a bomb threat, and then make sure you're the last one out of the office. Or try slipping a laxative into her tea and wait for her to scamper off to the restroom.

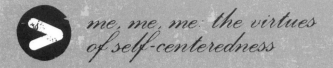

me, me, me: the virtues of self-centeredness

Why is it wrong to expect the whole damn world to revolve around you? It seems to work for the sun just fine. You're the center of the universe— it's a scientific fact—and the sooner everyone learns that the easier it'll be for all of them. It's time for Ego Astronomy 101. Teach your friends these modified Laws of Planetary Motion (the hard way, if necessary):

LAW #1
THE ELLIPTICAL LAW

In astronomy, this means that planets orbit around the sun elliptically. On Planet You, however, it means that everyone's life revolves around you and your interests. We don't quite understand the science of it—it has something to do with a sucking need so great that not even light can escape from it—but the mechanics are unimportant. What *does* matter is that friends and family scurry to meet your every whim. Is your cocktail glass getting dangerously low? Do your feet need massaging? Somebody had better step to it, because if they fall out of orbit, well, it's meteor mayhem.

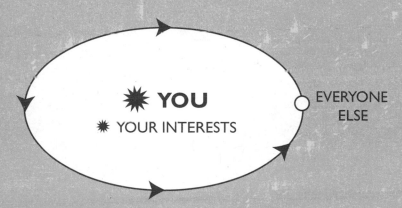

LAW #2
THE EQUAL AREAS LAW

This principle is more complicated. Basically, it has to do with a planet's radius vector sweeping out in equal areas at equal times in its orbit— oh, we can't even pretend we're interested in this stuff. Let's talk about how this law affects *you*. In a nutshell, it means that everyone needs to take quite seriously your need to be in a given place at the same time every day. Specifically, in front of the TV at 11:00 A.M. for *All My Children* and at Tony's Tavern at 5:00 P.M. for two-dollar PBRs and half-price hot wings. That means no poorly timed phone calls or requests to be driven to the hospital. Remember: if you don't get what you want when you want it, the whole space-time continuum could be affected.

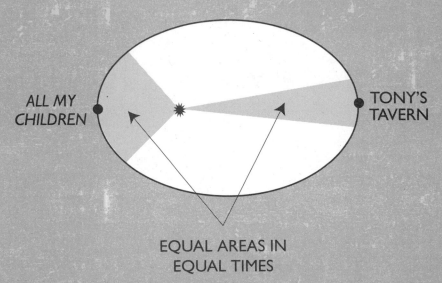

ALL MY
CHILDREN

TONY'S
TAVERN

EQUAL AREAS IN
EQUAL TIMES

LAW #3
THE HARMONIC LAW

This law of planetary motion relates the squares of two planets' revolutionary periods to the cubes of their semimajor axes, which apparently means something to people who didn't flunk ninth-grade science. Well, here's what it means to you: simply put, when you're happy, everyone's happy. And your happiness can be determined by the following formula:

$$\frac{P_1^{\,2}}{P_2^{\,2}} = \frac{R_1^{\,3}}{R_2^{\,3}}$$

P_1 = the number of cosmopolitans you are comp'd within an hour

P_2 = minutes spent waiting for your jalapeño poppers

R_1 = proximity of the nearest taco stand

R_2 = number of times your partner tells you how nice you look in those pants

PACK YOUR BAGS
GETTING THE MOST OUT
OF YOUR GUILT TRIP

Tell your friends and family to pack their bags, because you're taking them on a guilt trip. There's a bag for every occasion. Try these!

To manipulate . . .	**Use . . .**
Your partner	The "I always come last" duffel bag
Your siblings	The "Mom always liked you best" tote bag
Your parents	The "If you were around more when I was growing up I wouldn't have to rob convenience stores to get attention" clutch
Your friends	The "Sorry I can't get my shit together like you" suitcase

comportment: you can't take me anywhere

Good manners get you jobs, invitations, and in-laws. But who wants any of that? Learn to cultivate the bad manners that will ensure you don't get invited back to the events you didn't want to attend in the first place.

Baby Showers

Everybody hates baby showers, and with good reason. They take place at an hour normal people are still sleeping off a three-day bender. The very name implies liquid refreshment, and yet the offerings never seem to include anything stronger than Sanka. There's all that caring and sharing, all that oohing and aahing as the mother-to-be unwraps clothes that, while cute, are entirely too small to borrow. Well, baby, you've attended your last shower. Work these phrases into the conversation and you can be sure you'll never be invited to one again:

"I hope all that ecstasy she did in college didn't damage the baby's chromosomes."

"Yeah, I suppose her husband *could* be the father. I guess we'll find out soon enough!"

"It's nice that she was able to conceive after having so many abortions."

Potlucks

Who brought the moldy, week-old, half-eaten burrito? You did, *hombre*, and it's your one-way ticket to Never-Get-Invited-to-One-of-These-Lame-Dinner-Parties-Again-Ville. Bravo!

Sales Parties

It's not a party if you have to buy Tupperware, cosmetics, or "passion" products and are rewarded with overtired vegetables, watery dip, and flavored water. Your ticket out? Inappropriate questions about the products. Try one of these:

"Can you use this concealer below the waist?"

"How long will a stool sample stay fresh in one of these?"

"Now, can the nipple clamp also be used as a chip clip?"

Reunions

It worked in high school, and it'll work now. Vomit on a classmate at your tenth and you won't be asked back for your twentieth. You haven't changed a bit!

Weddings

Dirty dancing with the bride or groom will raise a few eyebrows, but it won't get you eighty-sixed from all future ceremonies. No, the lifetime blackball is to be found in the wildly inappropriate toast. So raise your glass, my friend, and prepare to use this golden line: "I've got a story I'd like to share. Now, this takes place back when the bride was still dating women ..."

MONEY AND & CAREER

What with the incapacitating hangovers and weeks hiding in Mexico from Johnny Q. Law, you'll find that the Retox lifestyle and keeping a job don't exactly go hand in hand. Unfortunately, neither do the Retox lifestyle and poverty. In a perfect world you'd be able to live off the winnings from your nuisance lawsuits, but for now you have to punch the clock. Not to worry, worker bee. We've got lots of ideas to make your workplace toxic in a *good* way. Treading the careful line between getting fired (bad) and getting promoted (also bad, because it probably means a lot more work for just a little more money), you'll be biting the hand that feeds you for years to come. We've also got lots of money-management ideas to make sure that paycheck covers the really important things, like lotto tickets and alcohol. *Trust in the abundance of the mini-mart.*

 *the retox savings plan*

If you're like most people, you don't give your financial future much thought. Who cares about 401(k)s and saving accounts when it's happy hour? And while it's true that buying half-price drinks is a great savings strategy, it's not quite enough. It's all too easy to spend all of your money buying doughnuts and wine coolers in the morning and be left with nary a dollar for your nightcap. That's why a little planning never hurt anybody. With these Retox money management techniques we'll make sure you're never left high and dry when it really counts.

The Purge Plan

We all have unused junk that we could turn into capital. Start by getting rid of your newspaper subscriptions, gym memberships, and garbage service. The first two you never use anyway (whom are you kidding?) and, as for the latter, you can always sneak your garbage into your neighbor's bin in the middle of the night. Now take the money, put it in a jar, mix up a batch of martinis, and just watch it grow (this may require up to five batches of martinis before you actually see anything happening). When you've got enough money saved, consider investing it. We recommend diversified funds like keno, video poker, and Pai Gow.

The Bingo Plan

They say less is more, but we say *more* is more. Buying in bulk is a great way to save some coin. By spending a little more money initially, you'll save a lot in the end. Buy boxes of wine, cases of candy bars, and cartons of cigarettes. If you're still hurting for money, try selling those extra cigs to underage kids for ten dollars a pack.

The Chutzpah Plan

You'd be surprised at how easily you can get out of paying for things if you just have the balls—and the quick hands—to make it work for you. Sure, you'll chip in for dinner with friends! First, make sure you have some cash on you. When the bill comes, simply put a ten down and take back two fives. No one will notice, and the poor sucker with the credit card will be forced to pick up your slack.

The Greedy Pig Plan

Viewing the company coffer as your own personal piggy bank seems to be a popular money management technique among top CEOs, and look how rich *they* are! Start with shady bookkeeping and move your way up to falsifying annual reports. Use this method only if you look good in orange.

YOU *DESERVE* IT
HANDY RATIONALIZATIONS
FOR OVERSPENDING

We've been told time and time again that it's how you feel on the inside that counts. And we couldn't agree more. Who can feel good on the inside when the outside is wearing last season's Dolce & Gabbana? Don't give yourself less than you deserve.

Here are some handy mantras to silence that little voice in your head that says you can't afford something:

"My card gives me miles."

"I can afford this if I don't eat."

"It's really more economical to buy the two-liter bottle."

"Everyone needs his own butler."

"This electric waxing kit will pay for itself."

"A classy pair of chaps never goes out of style."

"Buying my own tanning bed is cheaper than flying to the Bahamas."

"Anything but filet mignon makes the kitty sick."

"You can't put a price tag on self-esteem."

"I can declare bankruptcy once every seven years."

"Think of how much I'll save on groceries if I have my own personal chef."

"Plastic surgery is cheaper than a lifetime of therapy."

"A solid-gold doorstop reminds me that I'm *special*."

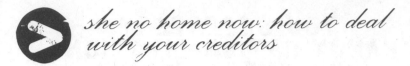

she no home now: how to deal with your creditors

Do you get more calls from your credit card company than you do from your family? Well, it makes sense—Visa and Mastercard gave you a lot more money. But that doesn't mean you have to cringe in fear every time you hear your phone ring. Reclaim your phone with these evasive debt management strategies.

No Speaky English

"¿Donde está la playa?" "¡Me gusta la helado!" We're not sure why we wasted so much time in high school Spanish class learning to ask for directions to the beach or express our affection for ice cream when there was only one sentence we really needed to know: "No está aquí." Repeat this handy phrase whenever a creditor gets you on the phone, throwing in an occasional "No comprendo inglés." If the caller actually speaks Spanish, switch to pig Latin Spanish and pretend it's Basque. *Adios*, sucker!

I Do Know Ka-razy

There's no way your credit card company will expect you to send in a check next week if you tell them you're going to be out of town, on planet Pikon 8. And a terrifying nonstop bout of logorrhea will ensure they don't call back for a good long time. Paranoid fantasies are particularly effective: "Did the CIA send you? Their transmitters are every-

where, they're in the faucet and they can read my mind when I brush my teeth. They want to kill me because I know too much about the kim chee affair. It's global, man, it's global, but it's OK, I've got the magic Pokémon protection amulet and they're all going down and they're taking you with them."

Daddy Can't Come to the Phone Now Because He's Crying

Even the most hardened bill collector won't yell at a child. If you don't have one, simply speak in a high, lisping voice. Ask, "Did my mommy do something bad?" then press some random keys and hang up.

Two Birds, One Stone

Insist you've been the victim of identity theft, taking care to point the finger at someone who's already on your shit list. If you're lucky, you'll get your debt forgiven and enjoy the satisfaction of knowing you sent a jerky, albeit innocent, person to the pokey.

Psychological Warfare

We know the credit card telephone representatives are just doing their job, but you're also just doing yours. And your job is to spend money you can't repay and then make the people hired to nag you for it weep in shame. Don't be afraid to make up a sick baby, a kitten who will probably need surgery, or a deceased spouse.

The Overshare

Remember: nothing ends an unwanted call faster than a blow-by-blow account of your recent colonoscopy.

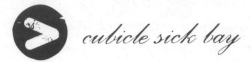 *cubicle sick bay*

After last night's tequila shooter marathon, we bet you're really kicking yourself for using up your sick days to stay home and watch the *Planet of the Apes* marathon. Well, what's done is done; nothing to do now but make the best of it. For days when you have to go to work and you'll be taking a hangover with you, here are some ways to make it as comfortable as possible.

Cubicle Quarantine

Your top priority: *to keep coworkers as far away as possible.* If they get near you, there's a chance they could give you something to do. "Stomach flu" is the magic phrase here. No one's afraid of catching a hangover, but rumors of a violent GI virus will ensure you're left completely alone all day. Drive the point home with some loud at-desk dry heaving and you'll guarantee yourself a work-free week.

Self-Inflicted Workers' Comp

There's nothing like a potential lawsuit to get yourself sent home early. Aim for a minor stapler accident or pushpin goring at the start of the day. There's no way a thumbtack puncture will hurt as much as your headache does, and in any case you're still so drunk you probably won't even feel it. So go ahead and let your index finger take one for the team. A day off is worth a missing fingernail.

Desk Chair Spin-Off

Chances are the cubicle will be spinning. See if you can't spin your chair fast enough to keep up with it. Oh, nope, bad idea; got that lined wastebasket handy?

Misery Loves Company

If you're like us, making others feel bad makes you feel better. Sure, it's not your coworkers' fault that you've got a skull-crushing hangover, but that's no reason not to spread the pain around. Moan relentlessly. Complain bitterly. Make snide comments about your coworkers' outfits and help yourself to the "coworker buffet" (see page 138) in the office refrigerator. Then shoot off a few nasty e-mail messages and call it a day.

Hair of the Dog

It's the official office mascot!

Office Canopy Bed

Until they invent a fully reclining desk chair, you're just going to have to make do by curling up under your desk. Think of it as an office canopy bed. And since that's where you'll be spending the better part of your morning, you want to make it comfortable. Keep a stash of pillows, lap quilts, and magazines on hand. For privacy, make a curtain from trash bags. It's not as good as spending the day lying on the couch, but at least you're getting paid.

SICK DAY EXCUSES

Everyone needs the occasional mental health day. Some of us need two or three a week. When you're calling in sick/indisposed/bereaved that often, you start to run out of excuses. If you've killed off Grandma more than once this year, we've got just what you need: a handy-dandy list of sick-day excuses. Disturbing enough to discourage further questioning, each one is a surefire get-out-of-work-free card. Enjoy!

Excuses for Not Coming to Work:

It's coming out of both ends.

I tripped over my cat and was knocked unconscious.

My testicles have swollen to the size of grapefruits.

Mom's trial starts today.

The sores have spread to my face.

Someone broke into my home and stole all my shoes.

I'm getting the boil on my ass lanced today.

I hit a deer on the way to work.

It burns like the fires of hell when I pee.

Excuses for Not Returning after Lunch:

I crapped my pants.

I was arrested for public nudity.

A flock of angry birds converged on me in the park.

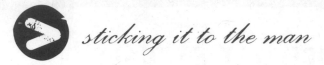
sticking it to the man

Unless you're working for a nonprofit, you're probably slaving away for a corporation that's conducting some type of shady business. If they're not exploiting poverty-stricken children in Asia or destroying the rain forest, they're probably funding South American guerrillas. Stealing office supplies is a great form of protest. Sure, you could just quit, but isn't it more noble and courageous to fight on the frontlines? Especially when it means you never have to buy toilet paper?

Do It for the Environment

Did you know that every day thousands of trees are clear cut and turned into pulp just so we can have paper towels, paper cups, paper plates, and the like? We're ruining our environment for a bit of convenience! Normally we're all for convenience, but we can take a stand when it suits our purpose. Instead of buying these products, steal them from your office. We realize this will not really save any paper, but do you expect us to be logical when we're this angry? Save the planet!

Do It to End Hunger

With so many starving people in the world, sometimes it just doesn't feel right to spend money on a tasty and fortifying lunch. And why should you, when you can steal your coworkers' lunches from the communal fridge? Start by taking only one item from each of a few select bags to assemble a delicious and nutritious meal, and gradually build up to wholesale lunch larceny. Your coworkers' involuntary donation will keep you satisfied and serve as a gentle reminder that a tiny sacrifice on their part can make the world a better place.

Do It for the Children

Most offices have a petty-cash jar for sundries like coffee, doughnuts, and the occasional office birthday party. But what about *your* kid's birthday party? Even if you don't have any children, you might someday, and the piss-poor salary they pay you sure won't cover such luxuries as cake and presents. Why should your kids go without? What did they ever do

to your boss? Start dipping into the company cash to ensure that your children will have the life they deserve.

Do It for Peace

Are you sick of arguing with your roommate or spouse over who paid what bill and who contributes more to the household? It's time to broker a truce. Every home needs some basics like tape, staplers, scissors, pens, and laptops, and by providing these at your company's expense you'll be spreading peace throughout your world. If you sniff the whiteout, you'll feel really, *really* peaceful.

AFTER-WORD

Congratulations! It's been a grueling process, but you've made it to the end. You've worked the program. You've kept on keepin' on. You've eaten your weight in hydrogenated trans-fatty acids, sipped a sea of gin, and inhaled a host of chemicals so toxic that they're banned even in former Soviet republics. *Nazdrovie,* Comrade Yeltsin!

Now, you're a whole new you. A greasy, out-of-shape, terrifically happy you. You've gone to seed. You know what seeds become, right? They become beautiful flowers. That's you, poppy. That's you.

But don't let it go to your head (that's the alcohol's job, silly!). Retox is an ongoing process, a commitment you renew every day. Every morning—well, every afternoon—that you wake up in a nest of your own filth in an apartment you don't recognize, you commit anew: Today, I will do what feels good, long after it starts feeling bad. I will eat what I want. I will medicate my emotions. I will manipulate the people I love. I will make mistakes, I will not learn from them, and I will not apologize.

The going may get rough. Sometimes you just won't feel like popping a Valium, downing a boilermaker, or violating the terms of your parole.

But you ll just have to push on through. Of course, you ll need to avoid the people and places that you associate with your former healthful lifestyle. We ve seen it a million times. You think, I ll just stick my head in Curves to make fun of those poor clueless suckers, and the next thing you know, you re wearing Reeboks and sipping Gatorade. Everyone has the occasional relapse. But when that happens, you just get back on that horse, and slide off the saddle into the gutter where you belong. And so it goes, one day at a time.

You ve got a lot of damage to do, so we ll turn you loose. You ve graduated, and it s time to do what all graduates must: get wasted, run around the parking lot naked, and embarrass your parents. That champagne won t dump *itself* over your brother s head, so go on now and lend it a hand.

To your health!